FREDDIE THE FROG AND FRIENDS

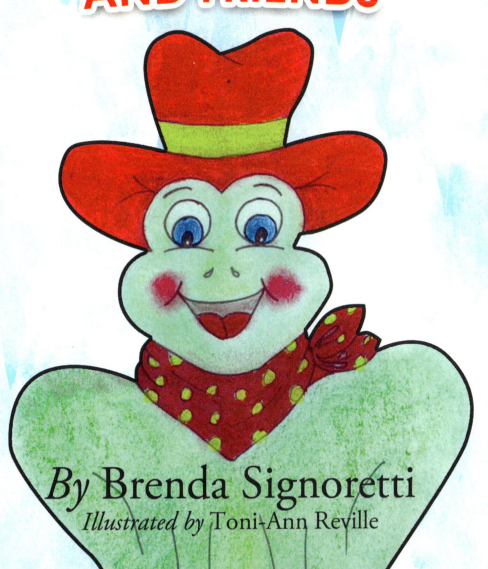

By Brenda Signoretti

Illustrated by Toni-Ann Reville

AuthorHouse™
1663 Liberty Drive
Bloomington, IN 47403
www.authorhouse.com
Phone: 1-800-839-8640

© 2011 Brenda Signoretti. All Rights Reserved.

No part of this book may be reproduced, stored in a retrieval system,
or transmitted by any means without the written permission of the author.

First published by AuthorHouse 09/26/2011

ISBN: 978-1-4634-4633-8 (sc)

Library of Congress Control Number: 2011913924

Printed in the United States of America

Any people depicted in stock imagery provided by Thinkstock are models,
and such images are being used for illustrative purposes only.
Certain stock imagery © Thinkstock.

This book is printed on acid-free paper.

Because of the dynamic nature of the Internet, any web addresses or links contained in this book may have changed since publication and may no longer be valid. The views expressed in this work are solely those of the author and do not necessarily reflect the views of the publisher, and the publisher hereby disclaims any responsibility for them.

Anthony the **a**nt **a**te **a**n **a**pple.

Cody the caterpillar can't crawl.

Hh

Harvey the **h**ippo **h**as a **h**eart.

Jj

Joseph the jaguar jumps in jello.

Ll

Lauren the lamb likes lillies.

Mm

Maddy the mouse makes a mess.

Oo

Owen the octopus plays the organ.

Pp

Peter the **p**ig **p**aints a **p**ole.

Qq

Qu**i**n**t**a the **qu**ail is a **q**ueen.

Rr

Robbie the **r**abbit **r**uns the **r**ace.

Sarah the **s**quirrel plays **s**occer.

Yy

Yola the **y**ak is **y**ellow.

CPSIA information can be obtained
at www.ICGtesting.com
Printed in the USA
253003LV00001B